香港國際詩歌之夜 *2015*
INTERNATIONAL POETRY NIGHTS IN HONG KONG

編輯 Editors

北島 Bei Dao

陳嘉恩 Shelby K. Y. Chan

方梓勳 Gilbert C. F. Fong

柯夏智 Lucas Klein

馬德松 Christopher Mattison

宋子江 Chris Song

English translations by Jami Proctor Xu

目錄 Contents

宋琳
Song Lin

憶故人

我牽掛的客人披著雪斗篷，
說他來自某個久遠，
從寒武紀，從伯吉斯頁岩
和刺胞動物的嘴，
經歷了最淒苦的流亡。
說他是我的同族，長著與我
相似的顴骨，濃濃的，糾在一起的眉毛。
他聲音柔美勝似當初。
我請他坐下，談談，
他脫口說出醉人的話語：

　　雪普降的天下鹽
　　我抽象地嘗了嘗。我的舌頭純化了
　　人對世界的終極評價
　　——甜。
　　夸克，那隻虛空的核桃，
　　我剝開它，
　　宇宙的心，就在黑雲母的
　　心中砰砰跳。
　　鶴，我的姐妹，

剛洗了澡，噴了點
彩虹牌香水，
正在夕照的那邊等著。
我寧願赤足蹈雪，
也不要偽裝成真理
混入永恒。

有福的人哪，勾魂家，
不可測度的親人，
在元詩礦山上熬煉著
雲、藥片和瀝青鈾裏的女巫，
他走過的離鄉路迤邐在長庚星的望遠鏡裏。
我問他那邊的清涼世界有甚麼不同，
雪花是否呼嘯，如酩酊的蝴蝶？
他緘默不語，並起身告別，
四周頓時彌漫奇異的薄荷香。
而話語的餘溫如三葉蟲的眼皮，
將埋入顱骨的脈狀礦床下，
封存在烏有鄉的失物招領處。
更多留給死亡破解的字謎，

漂浮著，被誤解，被流傳，
在大江南北。

Missing an Old Friend

The guest I was concerned about wore a snow cloak,
and said he'd come from some remote age,
from the Cambrian Period, from the Burgess Shale
    Formation
and the mouth of Cnidarian,
and that he'd been through the bleakest exile.
He said he was the same ethnicity as me
with a skull shaped like mine and thick, tangled
    eyebrows.
His voice was gentler than before.
I asked him to sit and talk,
and he blurted out intoxicating words:

    I've abstractly tasted the salt
    the snow has let fall onto the earth. My
        tongue purified
    people's final judgment of the world
    —It's sweet.
    The quark, that hollow walnut,
    I peeled it,

the universe's heart pounding
in black mica's heart.
My sisters, the cranes,
had just finished bathing, applied
a little rainbow perfume,
and were waiting in the sunset.
I'd rather step barefoot in the snow
than disguise myself as truth
to sneak into eternity.

The blessed, the seducer,
the unfathomable relative
is on the mine of metapoetry smelting
clouds, pills, and the witch in bituminous uranium.
The road of exile he'd traveled wound through the
     evening star's telescope.
I asked him what was different about the clear and
     cool world there,
did the snow whistle like drunken butterflies?
He kept silent and got up to leave.

A strange faint mint scent suddenly pervaded the air,
and the remaining warmth of our words was like a
    trilobite's eyelids—
to be buried beneath the vein-like deposits on the
    skull
and kept in the lost and found of nowhere.
More riddles for death to decipher—
floating, being misunderstood, and being retold
throughout the country.

脈水歌

—— 重讀《水經注》

1

大河在遠方閃爍，猶如一道
來自北極的光。太陽的火舌下
羿的箭矢穿過雲的旗幡
我移動，像《山海經》中的測量員
雁陣在藍天書寫一個人字
流水浣洗著林壑的耳朵
在我的衣襟前製造一個節日
飛瀑在懸崖絕壁激起回響
一條又一條河穿過我的軀體
帝國的通都和采邑中有我的驛站
美人因遲暮而憂傷，醒來
衣袖空留昨夜的餘溫

2

岸草青蔥尾隨我遠去
而生活本是在岸上築居
為甚麼要告別笙歌和畫舫
去追逐蠻荒的河流？
為甚麼騎驢，飲風，傴僂而進

易水而弱水，塞北又江南？
漫長的行旅中，孤獨已變成
心的刺客。夜半客船上
家書的爐炭烘暖我的雙手
出發的日子，話別的時刻而今安在？
兇年又加上不馴服的河道
星星的沙粒壅塞平原

3
死亡的黑車滿載兵器
烽火中的白馬連翩西馳
曙光像秘件的封泥那樣火紅
大河從貧瘠的遠方流來
經過同戰爭一樣貧瘠的土地
那麼多人在飢餓中死去，又在死後夢見
玉蜀黍和乾葡萄，夢見女人們雲集
辨認著比凍土更僵硬的自己
手在空中掘墓：蒼天！蒼天！
她們像懷中嬰兒般號叫

那麼多等待化為烏有
好似干戈化為玉帛

4
倘若青鳥來過，曾棲於甚麼枝頭？
羅盤搜尋到哪一座仙島或靈山？
裸國殘缺，怪物的想像同樣殘缺
龍族的血液裏有牠們的低語、尖叫
〈禹貢〉山水猶在，貢船早傾覆
接著走來了遊俠，縱橫家
和篡位者儀仗中大象雄武的步伐
這片土地的傳說，河流的傳說
像炭黑的赤壁被燒得滾燙
像石上的勒文，只有風能夠識讀
連同智者的浩嘆都將化為烏有
影子交錯，有誰曾抵達過彼岸？

5
漁父調舟而去，桂棹輕點
拋下一支惱人的〈滄浪歌〉

多事之秋的高樹用傷疤的瞎眼眺望
我走過的泥足深陷的路
一隻蝴蝶被塵土壓住有無原由？
一隻螢火蟲為我照明是否出於自願？
除了繼續早已開始的仰觀俯察
涇屬渭汭的清濁，南北分流的盤根錯節
現在豈不是一一稽考的時候？
說，即便最終等於不說
像流星的湮滅，石棺的沉默
鐵函有朝一日會浮出深井

6

雲夢澤上的雲，銷魂的雨
宋玉的解夢術滿足了楚王的淫慾
清水之畔，筑篁幽幽，名士們
佯醉、打鐵、冶遊於林中
與殘暴的君主曠日周旋
我又怎能幸免侍者的頭銜
在奉命陪同皇帝北巡的遊歷中
夢想山川風物和美的人心

從一部水之書發現了不得已之境
我豈不願放浪於市廛之間
像綠鸚鵡，在燭光的嫵媚中
在玄奧中談吐世道陵遲

7
開創的人物，天之驕子
遙遠如來自某個河外星系
沿著傾斜的日影下凡
敷土，祭奠高山，命名了百川
那傳說中的水王不曾回來
廣漠掩埋遲到者的悲哀
河與人喧響兩種孤寂
一如那不可能停下的箭矢
唯有脈跳還在呼應地下的湧動
唯有記憶匯合成更遼闊的河
當我躊躇著不知該向何處去
月亮那水的魂魄引導我

8

經典已撲散。在扭曲的時代
我只想做一個脈水人
在精心繪製的地圖上規劃
一度是桃花源，後來是戰場的山水
渴時我就以朝聖者的姿勢彎下腰
風像色情的山鬼挑逗我：
看啊，一切皆流。但重泉中
我的影子卻如如不動
變化多端的四季的儀表
漲落的水文，讓我徒然興嘆
並連連發問：甚麼樣的鉤沉索隱
可以追回遁走的暗流？

9

這是一則軼事，這是流亡
漫長的行腳從一個龍忌的字開始
只帶上很少的必需品
走著，一個人不僅可以夢見
爵祿、榮名、弄臣的粉墨
可以洗手不幹，可以懶臥

也可以遠走高飛。沒有禹跡
只有銀色的絲誕那徐緩蝸牛的
逶迤哲學。對我而言，遠
就是近；走，就是用交替的腳踵
量盡河流的長度，大地的幅員
停步倚杖，在峻湍邊看雲

10
急迫的鷹喉叫著，喉叫著，喉叫著
大地之鷹，展翅在雲端
那聲音像黃昏天空的一個亮點
神秘的河圖的一個疑點
像從殷墟飛來的傳奇的巫祝
戴著面具，發出預言：
「旅者，你該向視域外搜尋
在傾聽中配製魔咒的力量
你也該知道源頭的涓滴原本弱小
逆流而上即與那一脈活水為鄰
夢想的顛躓也是生活的顛躓
當大河上的彩虹橫絕遠空」

Song of Exploring the Waterways

—Rereading the *Commentary on the Water Classic*

1

The great river glistens in the distance
like an aurora. Yi's arrows pass cloud banners
under the sun's flamed tongue.
I move like a surveyor in the *Classic of Mountains
    and Seas.*
A formation of geese writes the ideogram for person
    in the blue sky
flowing water washes the ears of the forest ravine
and creates a holiday on the front of my silk robes.
The flying waterfall echoes over the sheer cliffs.
River after river passes by my body.
There are hitching posts for me in imperial Tongdu
    and Caiyi
The beauty mourns her faded youth, and when she
    awakens,
all that's left is last night's warmth in her sleeves.

2

Riverbank grasses and greenery follow me into the
    distance
yet life builds its home on the riverbank.
Why do we leave behind flute songs and pleasure
    boats
to chase the savage river?
Why ride a donkey, drink the wind, grow weary and
    enter
the Yi or Ruo Rivers, Sai Bei or Jiangnan?
On a long journey, loneliness becomes
the heart's assassin. At midnight on the passenger
    ship
the charcoal of letters from home warms my hands.
The day of departure, the moment of farewell, and
    where am I now?
Famine years and untamed rivers,
star sands congest the plains.

3

Death's black chariot is loaded with weapons.
White horses in beacon-fires gallop west in
    succession.
Dawn is the same blazing red as the seal on secret
    documents
The great river flows from the barren distance
passing an earth as barren as war.
So many have died in that hunger, and after they
    died,
dreamed of grapes and corn, dreamed of women
    gathering
to see themselves stiffer than frozen earth
Their hands dig graves in the sky: Heaven! Heaven!
They cry out like infants being held.
So many await to become nothingness
like weapons of war becoming jade and silk.

4

If the black messenger bird came, on which branch
    did it alight?
Which Immortal Island or Soul Mountain did the
    compass find?
When Naked Country is battered, monsters'
    imaginations are also battered
the dragon people's blood holds their whispers and
    screams
The mountains and rivers in *Yu Gong* still remain, but
    the boats with imperial offerings sank long ago
Then come the knights-errant, the strategists
and the bold elephant-like march of the usurpers
The myths of this land, the myths of this river
like the coal black Red Cliffs being burned
like engravings in stone only the wind can read.
Together with the deep sighs of sages, they will all
    become nothingness.
Shadows intertwine, yet who has been to the other shore?

5

The fisherman turns his boat around and departs,
    gently dipping the cassia oars
casting off an annoying Song of Cang Lang River
A tall tree in a troubled autumn looks over the scene
    with eyes of scars.
The road I walked where my feet sunk deep in the
    mud.
Was a butterfly crushed in the dust for no reason?
Does the firefly shine for me of its own will?
In addition to surveying the clear and muddy bend
where the Jing and Wei Rivers converge,
the complications of which flow north or south
how is now not the time to inspect them all one by
    one?
To speak, in the end, is the same as not speaking,
like a meteor's annihilation, the silence of the
    sarcophagus.
One day the metal letter will float up from the well.

6

The clouds above Yunmeng Lake, ecstatic rain
Song Yu's dream interpretation skills satisfied the King
  of Chu.
Clear water's edge, serene bamboo, literati gentlemen
feign drunkenness, forge iron, and go courting in the
  woods,
wasting time mingling with the cruel king.
How did I narrowly escape the title of attendant,
ordered to accompany the emperor north,
dreaming of scenic mountains and streams and
  beautiful hearts.
In a book of water I discover the boundary of coercion
How could I be unwilling to loiter in the market,
metaphysically talking about the decline of the times
like a green parrot in the charming candlelight?

7

The first human, the pride of heaven,
distant as if from another galaxy,
descended to this earth along the slanted sun shadow,
laying out soil, offering sacrifices on the mountain,
   and naming the hundred rivers
That mythic king of the waters has never returned.
Vastness buries the sorrow of those who came late.
Rivers and people resound with two kinds of
   loneliness
like the unstoppable arrow
only arteries echo underground surges,
only memories converge into wider rivers.
When I hesitate and don't know where to go
the moon, that water spirit, guides me.

8

The Classics have been altered. In a twisted age

I just want to be an explorer,

to plan on a meticulous map.

Once there was the Peach Blossom Land, then a
   battlefield terrain

thirsty I'll bend forward in a pilgrim's posture

and the wind will titillate me like an erotic mountain
   ghost.

Look, everything is flowing, but in the layers of the
   spring water,

my reflection seems motionless.

The appearance of the ever-changing seasons,

the fluctuating hydrology makes me gasp in vain with joy.

I ask again and again: what sort of lost references

can bring back the fleeting undercurrents?

9

This is an anecdote, this is exile.

A long trek beginning with a word the dragon deems
   taboo.

Only bringing a few necessities.

Walking, not only can one dream

of nobility, glory, and becoming a favored imperial
   servant,

he can also wash his hands of this and lie down,

or he can fly far away. There are no traces of Yu

there's only the silver thread giving birth to that slow
   snail's

winding philosophy. For me, distance

is closeness; walking is alternating the heels

to measure the length of the river, the area of the land.

Pausing my steps, leaning on my staff, I look at the
   clouds from the torrents.

10

The urgent eagle is calling, calling, calling.
The eagle of the earth spreads its wings in the clouds.
The sound is a bright spot in the dusk sky,
a dubious spot on the mysterious river chart
like the legendary shaman who flew from the Ruins
  of Yin
wearing a mask, offering a prophecy:
"Travelers, you should search beyond vision
and create the power of magic in listening
You should know the stream that comes from the
  source is weak at first,
but if you walk upstream, you'll get close to the
  flowing water.
Stumbles in dreams are stumbles in life
when the rainbow over the river cuts across the
  distant sky."

布洛涅林中

湖水的碎銀，在巴黎的左側
獅子座越過火圈。

松針，你的儀式道具。

風數你變灰的頭髮，
睫毛，影子凌亂的狂草。

槳，沉默之臂劃過藍天
兜著圈子，乾燥像孩童挖掘的沙井
在夢之岸坍塌下來。
呼吸與風交替著
串串水珠的松林夕照
掛上隱居者的閣樓。

巨人頭顱，無人授受
磨亮渡口的老鐘遠在西岱島，
敲打死囚的回憶。

火鶴，你渴慕的豎琴，
彈撥湖心。
彩虹裏盲目的金子揮霍著，
覆盆子的受難日，
林妖現身於馬戲團，
爻辭之梅酸澀，
沒有歸期。

從水圈到水圈，
星的王冠被夜叉擊碎。

鐵塔下邊走來一個亡命者。

In Bois de Boulogne

Broken silver on the lake; on Paris' Left Bank
Leo passes through a ring of fire.

Pine needles, your ceremonial props.

The wind counts your graying hairs,
your eyelashes, wild grasses with shadows in disarray.

Oars, those silent arms, paddle across the blue sky
moving in rings, dry as the wells children dig in sand
that collapse into the banks of dreams.
Breath alternates with wind
The pine forest at sunset with strings of dewdrops
hanging from hermits' attics.

No one accepts the giant's skull
The old clock at the polished ferry crossing is far
    away on the Île de la Cité,
ticking against death row memories.

Flamingo, the harp for which you thirst,
plucks at the lake's heart.
The blind gold in the rainbow is squandered,
the Good Friday of raspberries,
the forest monsters appear in the circus,
The sourness of the trigram's plums,
has no return date.

The crown of stars is smashed by yaksha,
from hydrosphere to hydrosphere.

A fugitive walks over beneath the iron tower.

秦始皇陵的勘探

七十萬奴隸的勞作算得了甚麼？
在驪山蒼翠的一側，他們挖，他們挖。
再重的巨石終比不上強秦的課稅，
撬不起的是公孫龍子的堅白論。

癡迷的考古學家在烈日下勘探，
且為我們復現出，無論過去、現在、
或將來，各種暴君的癖好：
生前的奢華，死後無限的排場。

七十萬奴隸，七十萬堆塵土。
上蔡的李斯還能到東門獵幾回兔子呢？
阿房宮固然華美，經不住一把火燒，
肉體的永存有賴於神賜的丹藥。

空曠的帝國需要一些東西來填滿，
需要堅貞的女人為遠征的夫婿而哭泣，
六國亡魂該聽得見長城轟然傾頹吧？
該知道，地獄之塔奇怪的倒椎體。

但這深處的死亡宮殿卻是有力的矩形！
在令人窒息且揣摩不透的中心，
我猜測，祖龍仍將端坐在屏風前，
等待大臣徐福從遙遠的渤海歸來。

而機關密布中的弩矢是否仍能射殺？
肱著身，模擬百川和大海的水銀，
柔軟且安詳地熟睡著，一朝醒來，
會不會吐出千年的蛇信嚙咬我們？

隔著木然的兵馬俑，在相鄰的坑道裏，
殉葬的宮女和匠人吸進了最後一口空氣。
封墓的瞬間，透過逆光，他幾乎看見
一隻側身的燕子逃過了滅頂之災。

2007/2

Exploring Emperor Qin Shihuang's Tomb

What does the labor of 700,000 slaves matter?
On the green side of Li Mountain they dug and they dug.
In the end, the heaviest boulders couldn't compare
   with the Qin's mighty levies.
What can't be pried open is Gongsun Long's *Discourse
   on Hardness and Whiteness*.

Obsessed archeologists explore under the scorching sun,
yet all that persists in the memory, whether past, present,
or future, are the various addictions of despots:
the lavishness while alive, the unbounded
   extravagance after they die.

700,000 slaves, 700,000 piles of dust.
How many more times can Li Si of Shangcai come
   and hunt rabbits at the East Gate?
The magnificence of the E'pang Palace can't even bear
   one burning.
The eternity of the flesh relies upon the cinnabar elixir
   the gods confer.

The empty empire needs some things to fill it;
it needs chaste women to weep for their husbands on
     expedition.
Shouldn't deceased souls of the six countries to hear
     the Great Wall's rumbling collapse?
They should know the strange inverted spine of hell's
     pagoda.

But the palace of death in this abyss is a powerful
     rectangle!
In its unfathomable suffocating center,
I'm guessing the Dragon Ancestor still sits upright
     before the imperial screen,
waiting for minister Xu Fu to return from the far off
     Bohai Sea.

But can crossbows still kill in dense institutional
     cover?
simulating the mercury of the rivers and seas,
waking one morning after such soft and serene sleep,

will it stick out a thousand-year-old forked snake
    tongue and bite us?

In a tunnel adjacent to the stoic Terracotta soldiers,
palace women and craftsmen buried with the dead
    inhaled their last breaths.
The instant the tomb was sealed, in the backlight, he
    could almost see
the profile of a swallow who'd escaped being buried
    alive.

2007/2

口信

如果明天，黑色艦隊從我的眼睛登陸
請在夢中為鴿子鋪好床
並囑咐牠把眼睛轉向東方

如果我化身犰狳，從侏羅紀趕來救火
請讚美用撥火棍款待牠的人

如果我結結巴巴像石頭
在寒冷的高地睡去
你要靈巧如流水，用一支歌把我淹沒

如果地球的聾耳朵在閃電的神經末梢
聽不見情人們悲傷的低語
請對他們説：要麼守著銀河示眾
要麼像海蛞蝓，自由地卷曲

如果綠衣人按響了門鈴，你要祝福他
數到七，我就從彩虹裏面出來

2010

Oral Message

If tomorrow the black fleet lands from my eyes,
in a dream please prepare a bed for a dove
and remind it to turn its eyes to the east

If I turn into an armadillo and come from the Jurassic
    fighting fires
please praise the person who provided the fire poker.

If I stammer like a stone
and fall asleep in the frigid highlands
you'll need to be as nimble as water, and submerge
    me in a song.

If the world's deaf ears on lightning's nerve endings
can't hear the sorrowful whispers of lovers,
please tell them: if we don't want to be exposed
    beside the Milky Way,
we'll roll up freely as sea slugs

If the person in green rings the doorbell, bless him,
then count to seven, and I'll come out from inside
   the rainbow.

2010

用詩占卜

用一個被棄絕的詞
從兇手那裏奪回的詞
顛倒卦象
雙手握住最下面那個爻
讓它動起來

將要來臨的,我們知道你

廣袤的夜,廣袤的無名
你,異鄉者,隕石形狀的人
站在初地的邊沿,如在十地
那裏一座艮山
刺破大氣層
一粒精子前來做客
進入橐籥

你召喚燈蛾,你召喚死者
你掘一口通向鹽池的井
你敲打恐龍蛋,從中
取出一封來自玄武紀的信

讀吧，讀給我們聽
我們知道
那結痂的祥瑞也是你的

用一個暗啞的詞
盛放你的聲音
把它拌入黏土，敷在傷口上
把星座的咒語也拌進去
眼睛的網所泄漏的
我們收在心的葫蘆裏

你，異鄉者，為我們占卜！

Poem Divination

Use a cast off word,
a word seized from assassins
Reverse the hexagrams,
hands grabbing hold of the bottommost line
Make it move

You who are about to come, we know you

Vast night, vast namelessness
You, person from another place, meteorite-shaped
    person
standing on the edge of the first realm as if in the ten
    realms
A mountain there
pierces the atmosphere
A sperm that has come to visit
enters the furnace bellows

You summon the moths, you summon the dead
You dig a well that leads to a salt pond

You crack a dinosaur egg, and pull from it
a letter from Black Tortoise
Read it, read it to us
We know
that scabby omen is yours as well

Use a silent word
to hold your voice
Mix it with clay, apply it to your wounds
Mix in the incantations of constellations
That which the net of the eye lets slip through
we will gather it in the heart's gourd

You, person from another place, divine for us!

宋琳，1959 年生於福建廈門，祖籍寧德。1983 年畢業於上海華東師範大學中文系。1991 年移居法國，曾就讀於巴黎第七大學遠東系，先後在新加坡、阿根廷居留。2003 年以來受聘於國內幾所大學執教，目前專事寫作與繪畫。著有詩集《城市人》（1987）、《門廳》（2000）、《斷片與驪歌》（2006）、《城牆與落日》（2007）、《雪夜訪戴》（2015）、《口信》（2015）；隨筆集《對移動冰川的不斷接近》（2014）、《俄爾甫斯回頭》（2014）；編有詩選《空白練習曲》（2002）。現任《今天》文學雜誌的詩歌編輯、《讀詩》主編之一及《當代國際詩壇》編委。宋琳曾獲得「鹿特丹國際詩歌節獎」、「上海文學獎」、「東蕩子詩歌獎」等。

Song Lin was born in Xiamen, Fujian in 1959. He graduated from East China Normal University in Shanghai in 1983 and in 1991 moved to France to pursue graduate work in Far Eastern Studies at Université Paris Diderot. He has since lived in Singapore and Argentina, taught at various universities in China from 2003, and currently writes and paints full-time. His poetry collections include *City Dwellers* (1987), *Vestibule* (2000), *Fragments and Farewell Songs* (2006), *The City Wall and the Setting Sun* (2007), *Visiting Mr. Dai on Snowy Nights* (2015), and *Oral Message* (2015). His essay collections include *Continuous Approaches to Moving Icebergs* (2014) and *Orpheus Looks Back* (2014). With the poet Zhang Zao, he edited the anthology *Blank Etudes* (2002). He is an editor for the journals *Today* and *Reading Poetry*, and serves on the editorial board of *Contemporary International Poetry*. He is a recipient of the Rotterdam International Poetry Award, the Shanghai Literature Award, and the Dong Dangzi Poetry Award.

出版 Publisher
香港中文大學出版社 The Chinese University Press

封面影像 Cover Image
北島 Bei Dao

出版日期 Date of Publication
二零一五年十一月 November 2015

國際書號 ISBN
978- 962- 996- 741- 3

香港國際詩歌之夜 2015 International Poetry Nights in Hong Kong 2015
主辦單位 Organizer
香港中文大學文學院 Faculty of Arts, The Chinese University of Hong Kong

協辦單位 Co organizers
香港中文大學中國文化研究所
Institute of Chinese Studies, The Chinese University of Hong Kong
香港中文大學出版社 The Chinese University Press
香港兆基創意書院 HKICC Lee Shau Kee School of Creativity
廣州時刻文化傳播有限公司 Moment Communications

贊助 Sponsors
香港法國文化協會 Alliance Française de Hong Kong
上海廿一文化發展有限公司 Shanghai 21 Culture Promotion Co., Ltd.
中國會 The China Club
香港文學出版社有限公司 The Hong Kong Literary Press Co. Limited
斑馬谷文化發展 (北京) 有限公司 Zebra Valley Culture Development

Printed in Hong Kong